SOMETHING HAPPENED AND I'M SCARED TO TELL

A Book for Young Victims of Abuse

Written by Patricia Kehoe, Ph.D.
Illustrated by Carol Deach

Patricia Kehoe, Ph.D., a clinical psychologist,
specialized in child and family treatment.
She also wrote *Helping Abused Children*.
Dr. Kehoe died in 1996, leaving these
two books as her legacy for children's
health and well-being.

Carol Deach is an award-winning artist
from Stanwood, Washington. Other books
she has illustrated for Parenting Press
include *It's MY Body*, *Loving Touches*, and
My Grandma Died.

ISBN 0-943990-28-9 paper
ISBN 0-943990-29-7 library binding
LC 86-62032

Parenting Press, Inc.
P.O. Box 75267
Seattle, WA 98175

Introduction

This book is written for the very young child, ages three to seven, who is a suspected victim of sexual or physical abuse. It is not designed to prevent abuse or to substitute for intensive psychotherapy with these children. What it can do is encourage child victims to speak out, and give them the concepts that will help their recovery.

In my work with abused children, we return over and over to their damaged self-esteem and feelings of isolation and worthlessness. It is very difficult for one person to communicate to a child that he or she is not alone or at fault in these problems. That is how and why this book was written.

The story focuses on rebuilding the very fragile self-image of the young child. Reading it with a caring adult may be the beginning of a change in the way the child views himself or herself. I hope that this book will be useful to the many dedicated people, from parents to caseworkers to mental health professionals and attorneys, who help abused children reclaim their right to a childhood.

Something happened to me. I don't know just what
it was...and I don't know what to do.

Can I help?

Oh hi Lion. No, I don't want to talk about it.
Anyway, he told me not to tell...or else. Or else
nobody would love me anymore and my mommy
would send me away.

GRRR. Some grownups tell lies to make children keep scary secrets. Those mean things are **not** true. Somebody was just scared that you would tell the truth. Sometimes they say they won't be your friend anymore. Sometimes they say they'll hurt you. They say whatever will make you feel bad about telling.

When my brother gets a beating they say he's bad.
If I'm bad, I'll get hit too. Do you think I'm bad?

Of course not! Some things can never be a kid's fault, not ever! Being hurt by somebody else doesn't make you bad. Lots of kids feel mixed up about that.

What will really happen if I tell? Nobody will want
to play with me or be my friend, right?

Sure we will!
You are still the one and only,
very best you.

You see! It's not your fault. Some kids get hurt by hits and some kids get scared by the wrong kind of touches. But if you can talk about it, you can find grownups who will do their best to make those scary things stop. You just have to tell the truth.

But who can I tell?

You tell and tell until SOMEBODY listens. Start with your mom. If you can't tell her, tell someone you trust. You could talk to your teacher...or your doctor...or your neighbor...or your grandma or grandpa...or even your best friend's mom. You can tell me too, if you want.

Well, he touched me different, you know, not like fun hugs and kisses, not in front of people. It felt funny and scary too. But I don't get spanked anymore and if I let him do it, sometimes I get toys. It was under my pants, you know.

Those places have names—just like all the other parts of your body. Girls and women each have a vagina. Boys and men each have a penis. In back, everybody has an anus, just the same for boys and girls.

Talking about it makes me cry inside.

Everybody feels like crying when they are sad, hurt
or mad. It can help you feel better to cry on the
outside sometimes too.

Sometimes I still like him and sometimes I just feel so mad. I wish he would get run over dead by a car. Why did he do that stuff to me?

That stuff happens for a lot of reasons and none of those reasons are your fault. Kids can't always make a grown up stop doing things that they don't like. Maybe that's why you feel so mad.

This thing that happened to me. What's its name?

It's called sexual abuse and it can happen with anybody. Sometimes it's a parent, Grandad or Aunt who loves you, but gets mixed up about the right way to show it. Sometimes it's a stranger who is afraid to love other grownups. It can even be a big kid who wants to learn about sex but is afraid to ask about it.

But, how about when my brother gets hit?

When kids get hit so hard that it leaves a mark, or when they get hit all the time, or when they get in trouble so much they think nobody loves them, it's another kind of abuse. It happens when grownups get mixed up about how to show their mad feelings. They don't know how to be mad without hitting.

I don't ever want any more love. YUK!

Hey, wait a minute! There are all kinds of ways to show love. Some ways are just right for children, like hugs and cuddles. And some are just right for two grownups who love each other, like sex. Some grownups need to learn good ways to show their love and their mad feelings. It doesn't have to hurt!

Hey, it wasn't so bad talking to you after all. I do feel a little tiny bit better. I think I'll start to tell somebody now.

Grrrrreat! You sure are brave and I'm very proud
of you. Yucky feelings don't go away all at once,
but talking about them sure can help.

What about you? Who could you tell if something happened to you?

Guidelines for Reporting Suspected Child Abuse:

1. **Talk with the child.** Listen. Ask general questions until you are sure you understand what the child intends for you to know. It is not necessary to get a detailed statement because this will be obtained later under careful legal guidelines.

2. **Believe the child.** Let the child know that telling you about the abuse is a good thing to do.

3. **Reassure the child.** Let the child know that you still love, like or care for him. Tell him that you will do everything you can to help, but make only those promises you know you can keep.

4. **Call CPS or the Police.** Your local child abouse hotline is often the easiest place to start. Trained personnel can usually help you through the steps of the legal system. Remember that only *reasonable suspicion* of child abuse is required. You do not have to prove that it occurred before reporting your concerns.

5. **Protect the child's privacy.** Don't try to make the child confront the abuser or her parents immediately. Let the child talk to investigators before taking other action.

6. **Get support for yourself.** CPS usually maintains a list of mental health professionals and support groups who work with sexual abuse. City and county psychological and psychiatric associations, Family Service agencies and Child Guidance clinics are other resources.

More Books to Help Protect Children

It's My Body, by Lory Freeman and illustrated by Carol Deach, teaches children how to distinguish between "good" and "bad" touches, and how to respond appropriately to unwanted touches. Useful with 3-8 years, 32 pages, $5.95 paper, $15.95 library

Mi Cuerpo Es MIO, Spanish translation of *It's MY Body.* $7.95 paper

Protect Your Child from Sexual Abuse, by Janie Hart-Rossi offers parents information about sexual abuse and what to do to prevent child abuse. Useful with 1-12 years, 64 pages, $8.95 paper, $17.95 library

Loving Touches, by Lory Freeman and illustrated by Carol Deach, teaches children how to ask for and give positive and nurturing touches. Children also learn how to respect their own and other's bodies. Useful with 3-8 years, 32 pages, $6.95 paper, $15.95 library

Telling Isn't Tattling, by Kathryn Hammerseng and illustrated by Dave Garbot, helps children learn when to tell an adult they need help, and when to deal with problems themselves. Adults learn when to pay attention to kids' requests for help. Useful with 3-8 years, 32 pages, $6.95 paper, $15.95 library

The Trouble with Secrets, by Karen Johnsen and illustrated by Linda Johnson Forssell, shows children how to distinguish between hurtful secrets and good surprises. Useful with 3-8 years, 32 pages, $6.95 paper, $15.95 library

El Problema Con Los Secretos, Spanish translation of *The Trouble with Secrets.* $7.95 paper

Something Happened and I'm Scared to Tell, by Patricia Kehoe, Ph.D. and illustrated by Carol Deach, is the story of a young sexual abuse victim who learns how to recover self-esteem. Useful with 3-7 years, 32 pages, $6.95 paper, $15.95 library

Algo Pasó y Me Da Miedo Decirlo, Spanish translation of *Something Happened and I'm Scared to Tell.* $7.95 paper

Helping Abused Children, by Patricia Kehoe, Ph.D. provides many ideas and activities for care givers working with sexually abused children. Useful with 3-12 years, 48 pages, $10.95 paper, $18.95 library

Something Is Wrong at My House, by Diane Davis and illustrated by Marina Megale, offers children in violent homes ways to cope with the violence. Useful with 3-12 years, 40 pages, $6.95 paper, $15.95 library

Algo Anda Mal En Mi Casa, Spanish translation of *Something Is Wrong at My House.* $7.95 paper

Kids to the Rescue!, by Maribeth and Darwin Boelts and illustrated by Marina Megale, uses an interactive "what-would-you-do-if?" format, and prompts kids to think wisely in an emergency. Useful with 4-12 years, 72 pages, $8.95 paper, $18.95 library

---

Ask for these books at your favorite bookstore, call 1-800-992-6657, or visit us on the Internet at www.ParentingPress.com. Visa and MasterCard accepted. A complete catalog available upon request.

Parenting Press, Inc., P.O. Box 75267, Seattle, WA 98175
In Canada, call Raincoast Book Distribution, 1-800-663-5714

Prices subject to change without notice